D1441879

Peyton Manning

by Josh Gregory

Consultant: Barry Wilner
AP Football Writer

BEARPORT
PUBLISHING

New York, New York

Credits

Cover and Title Page, © AP Photo/Jack Dempsey; 4, © AP Photo/Mark Humphrey; 5, © AP Photo/David Drapkin; 6, © AP Photo/David Drapkin; 7, © Robbins Photography; 8, © Robbins Photography; 9, © AP Photo/Paul Spinelli; 10, © AP Photo/Ed Reinke; 11, © Robbins Photography; 12, © AP Photo/Adam Nadel; 13, © Robbins Photography; 14, © AP Photo/Tom Strattman; 15, © Robbins Photography; 16, © Robbins Photography; 17, © Robbins Photography; 18, © AP Photo/Ed Andrieski; 19, © Robbins Photography; 20, © Robbins Photography; 21, © Robbins Photography; 22, © Robbins Photography.

Publisher: Kenn Goin
Senior Editor: Joyce Tavolacci
Creative Director: Spencer Brinker
Photo Researcher: Josh Gregory
Design: Emily Love

Library of Congress Cataloging-in-Publication Data

Gregory, Josh.
  Peyton Manning / by Josh Gregory ; consultant, Barry Wilner, AP Football Writer.
    p. cm. – (Football stars up close)
  Includes bibliographical references and index.
  ISBN 978-1-62724-543-2 (library binding) – ISBN 1-62724-543-X (library binding)
 1. Manning, Peyton–Juvenile literature. 2. Football players–United States–Biography–Juvenile literature. 3. Quarterbacks (Football)–United States–Biography–Juvenile literature.
 I. Wilner, Barry. II. Title.
  GV939.M289G74 2015
  796.332092–dc23
  [B]
                                    2014029059

For more information, write to Bearport Publishing Company, Inc., 45 West 21st Street, Suite 3B, New York, New York 10010. Printed in the United States of America.

10 9 8 7 6 5 4 3 2 1

Contents

The Pressure Is On

On February 4, 2007, the Indianapolis Colts faced off against the Chicago Bears in **Super Bowl** XLI (41). The Bears earned a quick lead by scoring a **touchdown** on the very first play of the game. Colts **quarterback** Peyton Manning knew he would need to help his team even the score. Would he be able to rise to the challenge?

A Bears player makes the first touchdown. The early touchdown was the fastest score in Super Bowl history. It happened about 14 seconds into the game!

Peyton prepares to pass the ball as a Bears player rushes toward him during the 2007 Super Bowl.

The February 4, 2007, game was Peyton's first Super Bowl.

Super Bowl Hero

Peyton knew exactly how to take back control of the game. A few minutes after the Bears' touchdown, he threw an incredible 53-yard (48.5 m) touchdown pass to teammate Reggie Wayne. The Colts were back on track! For the rest of the game, Peyton was on fire. He completed 25 out of 38 passes and gained 247 yards (226 m). His fantastic plays helped lead the Colts to a 29–17 win. Peyton and his teammates were **NFL** champions!

Peyton (#18) looks down the line of players during Super Bowl XLI.

Peyton celebrating his Super Bowl win

Peyton was named Most Valuable Player (MVP) of Super Bowl XLI.

Like Father, Like Sons

Peyton grew up in a football family. He was born on March 24, 1976, in New Orleans, Louisiana. His father, Archie Manning, was a quarterback for the New Orleans Saints. Peyton and his two brothers wanted to follow in their father's footsteps. Archie encouraged all three of his sons to play football. He practiced with them and taught them the skills they would need to be great players.

Peyton (left) and his two brothers, Eli (center) and Cooper (right)

Peyton's younger brother, Eli, became a star quarterback for the New York Giants in 2004.

Archie Manning warms up before a game in 1981.

School Days

In high school, Peyton became the biggest star on the football team. During his three seasons as a **starting** quarterback, the team had an amazing 34–5 record. Peyton was known for throwing long, **accurate** passes. This helped him become one of the best high school quarterbacks in the nation. After graduating, he attended the University of Tennessee. There, he led the team to one win after another and set 33 passing records.

As a college player, Peyton looks for an open receiver during a 1995 game against the University of Kentucky.

Peyton threw 89 touchdown passes in college.

Peyton's large size helps him **fend off** tackles. He is 6 feet 5 inches (2 m) tall and weighs 230 pounds (104 kg).

A Rough Start

Many NFL teams wanted Peyton to play for them. However, Peyton was chosen by the Indianapolis Colts in the 1998 NFL **draft**. The Colts had won only three games during the previous season. The team was counting on Peyton to help them turn things around. Peyton played well during his **rookie** year. Still, the Colts lost several very close games and finished with a 3–13 record. Peyton was disappointed. He knew he would have to help his team do better next season.

Peyton proudly holds up his Colts jersey.

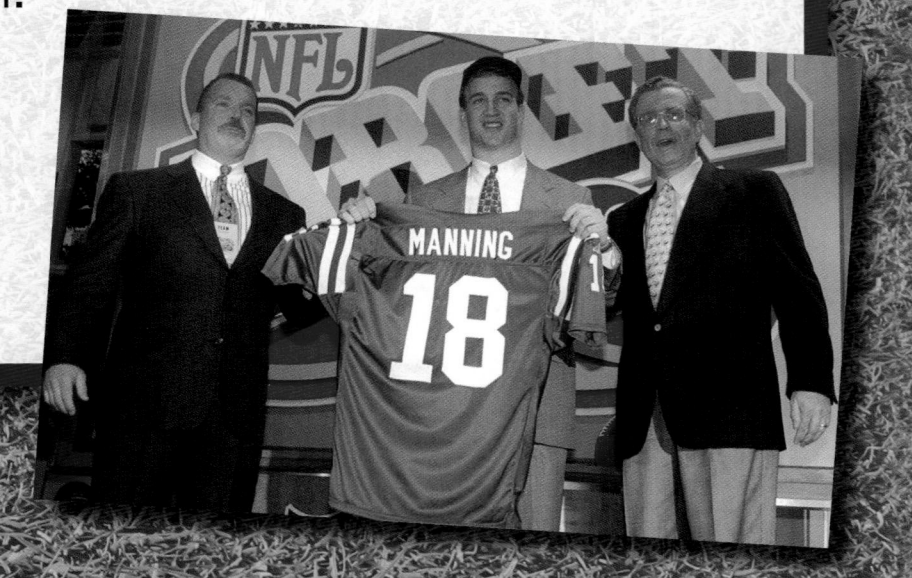

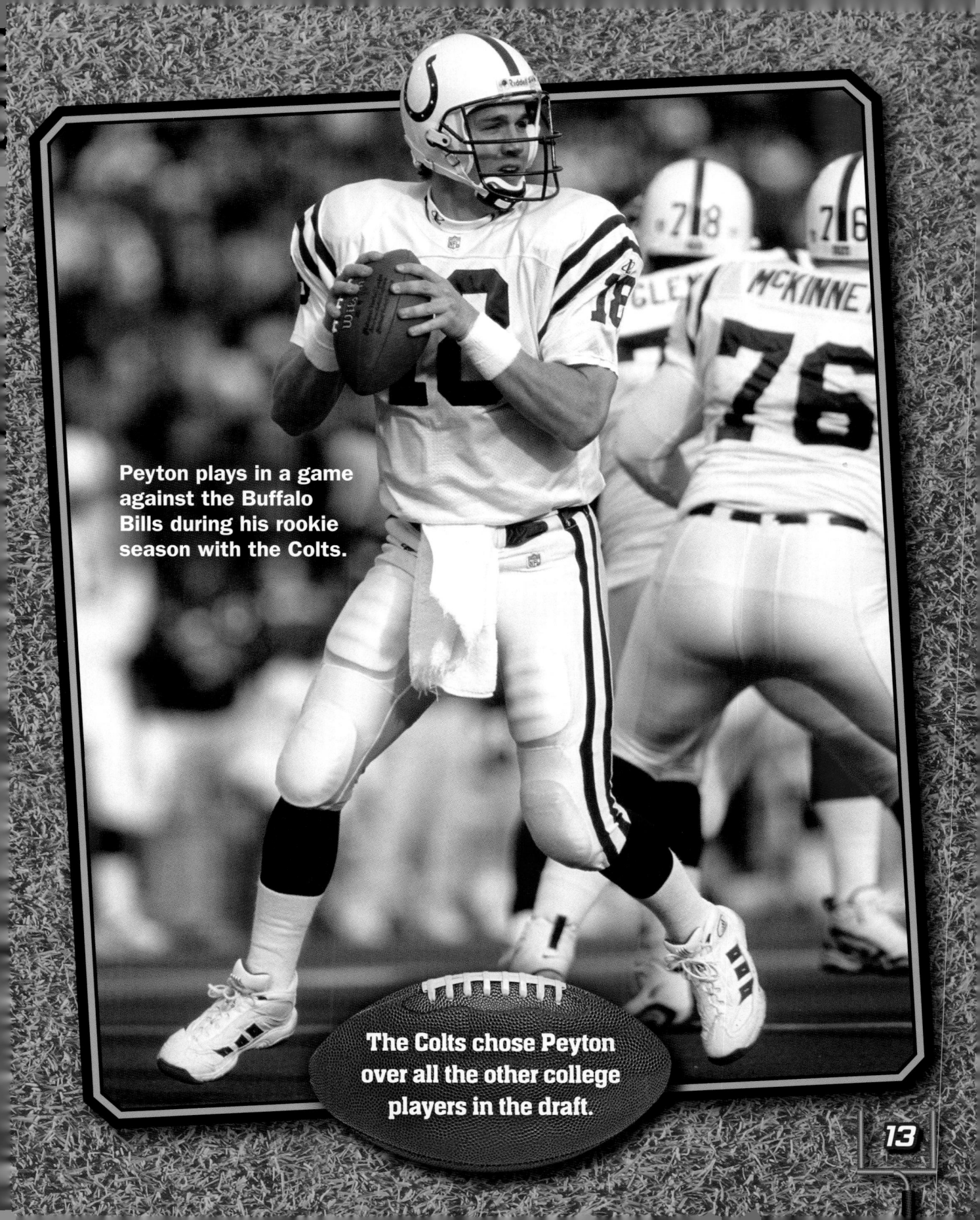

Peyton plays in a game against the Buffalo Bills during his rookie season with the Colts.

The Colts chose Peyton over all the other college players in the draft.

Terrific Turnaround

The 1999–2000 season was a big year for Peyton and the Colts. That year, Peyton was really able to show off his skills. The team kicked things off with a **victory** over the Buffalo Bills and went on to a 13–3 record. They even made it to the **playoffs**, though they were defeated by the Tennessee Titans. Peyton's incredible passing and strong leadership were an important part of the team's turnaround.

Peyton dodges a defender in a 1999 game against the Kansas City Chiefs.

Peyton threw 26 touchdown passes during the 1999–2000 season.

The Colts had gone through a weak 1998–1999 season. In the 1999–2000 season, thanks to Peyton, they had the strongest **comeback** in NFL history.

Becoming a Superstar

Peyton was quickly becoming one of the biggest stars in the NFL. Over the next few years, he led the Colts to two Super Bowls and won four MVP awards. Fans were amazed as they watched Peyton help the Colts win dozens of games. However, Peyton's successful streak didn't last. In 2011, he found out that years of playing football had injured his neck. He had to have **surgery** to fix it.

Peyton helps lead the Colts to a 24–20 victory over the Pittsburgh Steelers in 2008.

Peyton has thrown more touchdown passes than any other quarterback in NFL history.

Peyton was chosen to play in the **Pro Bowl** 13 times between 1999 and 2013.

On the Sidelines

After surgery, Peyton's neck took a long time to heal. He had to sit out the entire 2011–2012 season. The Colts were unsure if Peyton would ever be able to throw as well as he used to. So the team decided to replace him with a new quarterback. Peyton was upset, but he didn't give up on football. He decided to join the Denver Broncos.

Peyton holds up his new Broncos jersey.

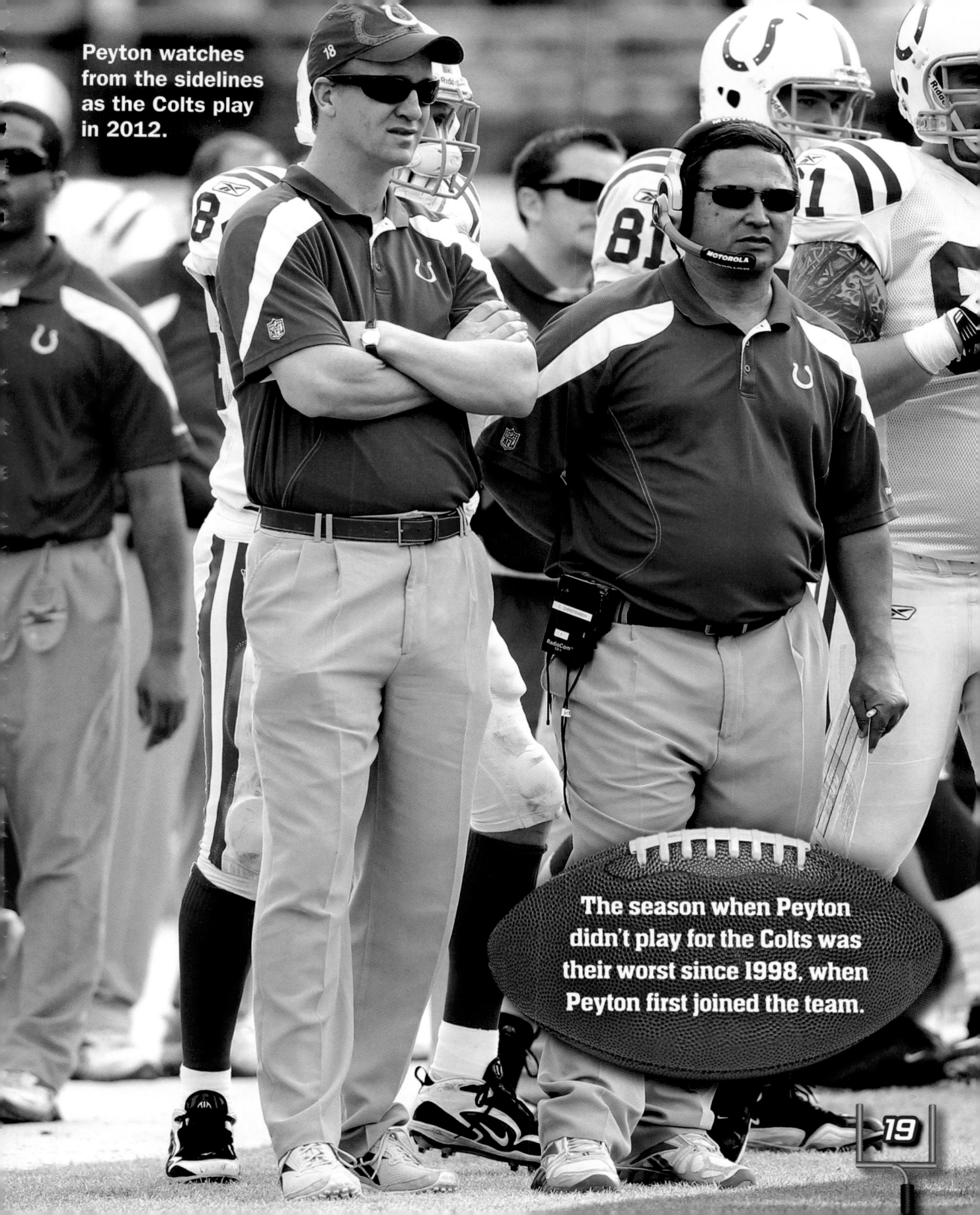

Peyton watches from the sidelines as the Colts play in 2012.

The season when Peyton didn't play for the Colts was their worst since 1998, when Peyton first joined the team.

A Strong Comeback

Fans wondered whether Peyton would be able to make a strong comeback. In his first season with the Broncos, Peyton led the team to a 13–3 record and to the playoffs. The next season was even better. Peyton broke the NFL record for most touchdown passes in a season. Best of all, he helped the Broncos reach the Super Bowl! After the difficulties of 2011, Peyton had proved that he was still a superstar player!

Peyton's incredible passing helped him win his fifth NFL MVP award in 2013.

Peyton gets fired up before a play in the 2014 Super Bowl.

Peyton Manning is the only player ever to win more than three NFL MVP awards.

Peyton's Life and Career

★ **March 24, 1976** Peyton Manning is born in New Orleans, Louisiana.

★ **1994** Peyton starts college at the University of Tennessee.

★ **1998** Peyton is drafted by the Indianapolis Colts.

★ **1999** Peyton is chosen to play in the Pro Bowl for the first time.

★ **2003** Peyton wins his first NFL MVP award.

★ **February 4, 2007** Peyton leads the Colts to victory in the Super Bowl.

★ **2009** Peyton wins his fourth MVP award.

★ **2011** Peyton has surgery to fix a neck injury.

★ **2012** Peyton joins the Denver Broncos.

★ **2014** Peyton wins his fifth NFL MVP award and breaks the NFL's record for most touchdown passes.

Glossary

accurate (AK-yuh-ruht) on target; free from mistakes

comeback (KUHM-bak) a recovery from a bad situation

draft (DRAFT) an event in which professional football teams take turns choosing college athletes to play for them

fend off (FEND AWF) to resist or defend against something

MVP (EM-VEE-PEE) letters standing for most valuable player; an award given to the best player in a game or in a season

NFL (EN-EFF-ELL) letters standing for National Football League, which includes 32 teams

playoffs (PLAY-awfss) the games held after the regular football season that determine which two teams will compete in the Super Bowl

Pro Bowl (PROH BOHL) the NFL's all-star game played by the season's best players

quarterback (KWOR-tur-bak) a football player who leads the offense, the part of the team that moves the ball forward

rookie (RUK-ee) a player in his or her first season in a sport

starting (START-ing) being the coach's first choice to play in a game

Super Bowl (SOO-pur BOHL) the final championship game of the NFL season

surgery (SUR-jur-ee) an operation performed to fix a part of the body

touchdown (TUHCH-doun) a score of six points that is made by getting the football across the other team's goal line

victory (VIK-tuh-ree) a win

Index

Bibliography

Official site of the Denver Broncos: www.denverbroncos.com

Official site of the NFL: www.nfl.com

Official site of Peyton Manning: www.peytonmanning.com

Read More

Sandler, Michael. *Peyton Manning and the Indianapolis Colts: Super Bowl XLI (Super Bowl Superstars)*. New York: Bearport (2008).

Savage, Jeff. *Peyton Manning (Amazing Athletes)*. Minneapolis, MN: Lerner (2008).

Wilner, Barry. *Peyton Manning: A Football Star Who Cares (Sports Stars Who Care)*. Berkeley Heights, NJ: Enslow (2011).

Learn More Online

To learn more about Peyton Manning, visit
www.bearportpublishing.com/FootballStarsUpClose